S T E V E

Michigan's
Upper
Peninsula

Spirit
of Place

by

B R I M M

Michigan's Upper Peninsula
Spirit of Place by Steve Brimm

Published by Tidal Creek Press

Photography by Steve Brimm

Book design and layout
Steve Brimm &
Matt Baumgardner - www.mattbaumgardner.com

Email: steve@brimmages.com
www.brimmages.com

ISBN: 0-9753971-0-9
First edition April 2004
Printed and bound in
Korea by
www.asianprinting.com

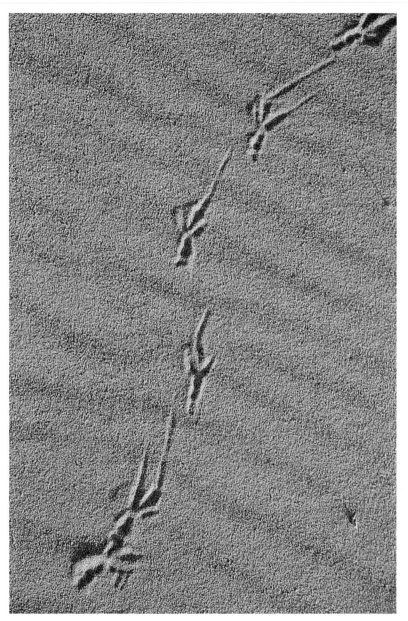

Above: Crow Tracks, Grand Sable Dunes, Pictured Rocks National Lakeshore
Page 1: Dead Spruce at Sunset, Lake Superior
Page 2-3: White Birch, Huron Mountains
Page 5: Autumn Storm, Lake Superior, Keweenaw Peninsula
Page 6: Black Capped Chickadee

Introduction

As my finger traced across the map following the shoreline, I tried to visualize the places as their names echoed in my mind. There was lots of green space on the map and what seemed like an eternity of water nearly surrounding an isolated peninsula. It looked like a place that could be called home.

At the time, the Colorado high country was where my snowshoes hung and even though I loved the mountains, water was calling me. Growing up in southeastern coastal North Carolina, most days possible were spent fishing, sailing and surfing. I wanted to get back to the water. However, it wasn't the Atlantic calling, it was Lake Superior. So, in true vagabond fashion, I grabbed my old camera, loaded my van and headed for an inland sea.

Like most amateur photographers, I wanted to capture on film the beautiful places that I saw. I m not exactly sure when I started to get serious about photography. Being entirely self-taught was certainly the long way around, but I believe the unhurried time spent learning allowed me to develop a unique style. I concentrate on light, texture & color as well as the juxtaposition of all three, rather than simply finding a subject to photograph. Although I'm called an 'artist', I feel that nature is the artist & that I simply interpret it's beauty. This respect for the natural world reflects my deep-rooted affection for the land, which hopefully is evident in the images I capture on film.

I have been photographing the Upper Peninsula for about twelve years now, and have been sharing some of those images with you at galleries, art shows and exhibitions. During that time quite a few folks have asked when I would put a collection my work together in book form. It's taken a while, but here it is.

Although I have lots of wonderful images from the whole lake Superior basin I chose to focus on my home — the U.P. Rather than show images of more notable and easily accessible features, I chose images that remind us of the whole, such as a loon wailing in the distance, a summer shower, a storm rolling across the big lake or the quiet of a winter wood. I hope to leave you with a feeling, somewhat intangible, but forming an impression all the same — like a fleeting chickadee on film.

My hope is that your journey through these images will allow you to feel what I have felt when hiking, paddling or sitting on a sunny outcropping — a sense of wonderment and a spirit of place.

As usual, my camera will continue to tag along on trips to places on the map that drew my finger to them years ago, which I now no longer have to visualize.

—*Steve*

Sandstone cliffs, Pictured Rocks National Lakeshore

Wood Lilly

Horseshoe Harbor Nature Conservancy site, Lake Superior

Bond Falls detail

West Branch Huron River

Flowering Bunchberry

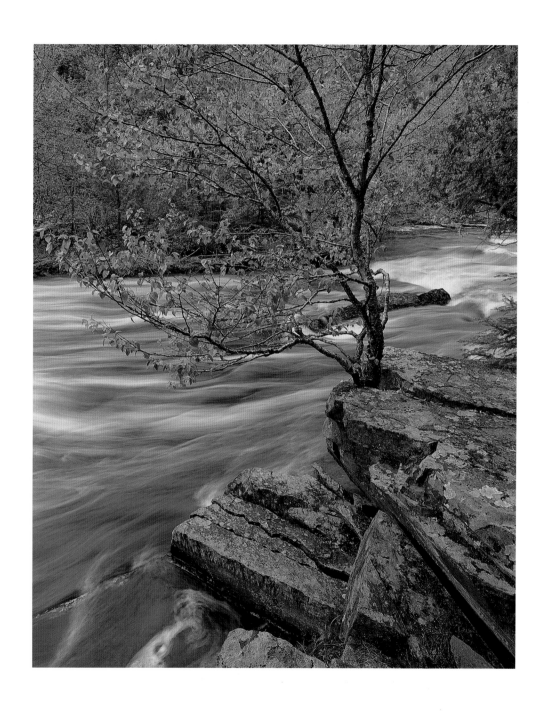

Sturgeon River, Canyon Falls recreation area

Red Pine Forest, Song Bird Trail

Arch Island, Lake Superior

Great Horned Owlet

Aspen and carpet of Trillium

Blue Flag Iris

Common Loon

Common Loons

Escarpment Trail, Porcupine Mountains Wilderness State Park

Lupine

Golden Eagle in Flight, Brockway Mountain

Conglomerate Shoreline, Lake Superior

Water Lilies, Seney National Wildlife Refuge

Painted Turtle, Seney National Wildlife Refuge

Minong Ridge, Isle Royale National Park

Pine Stump, Lake Superior

Grand Sable Dunes, Pictured Rocks National Lakeshore

Moonrise, Scoville point, Isle Royale National Park

Stone Beach, Whitefish Point

Clearing Storm, Middle Island Point

Basalt Beach Detail, Edwards Island, Isle Royale National Park

Cemetery Island, Isle Royale National Park

Top left clockwise: Black Bear, Moose cow and calf, Albino White-tailed Dear, Red Fox

Sparing Bull Moose, Isle Royale National Park

Astor Growing from Crack in Shale, Porcupine Mountains Wilderness State Park

Mosquito Beach Area, Pictured Rocks National Lakeshore

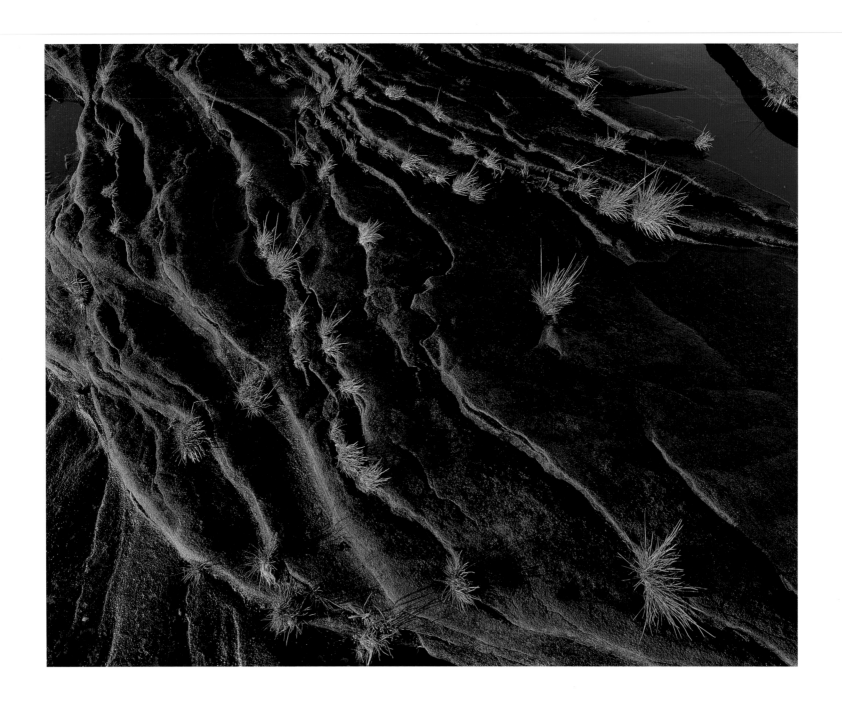

Sandstone and Grass, Point Abbaye

Rock Harbor, Isle Royale National Park

Bald Eagle, Seney National Wildlife Refuge

Lightning, Lake Superior

Sunset, West Caribou Island, Isle Royale National Park

Storm front with Mammatus Clouds, Lake Superior

Iron Stained Basalt, Presque Isle Beach, Lake Superior

Mineral Stained Sandstone, Pictured Rocks National Lakeshore

Lake Ritchie, Isle Royale National Park

Worn Sandstone and Pebbles, Five-mile Beach, Keweenaw co.

49

Grand Sable Dunes, Pictured Rocks National Lakeshore

Tamarack Bog

Miners Beach, Pictured Rocks National Lakeshore

Moonrise over Islets, Isle Royale National Park

River Detail, South Branch Ontonagon River

Fall Color Reflected around Falls, South Branch Ontonagon River

Sand Hill Crane

Wild Blueberry in Autumn Color, Seney National Wildlife Refuge

Big Carp River from Escarpment Trail, Porcupine Mountains Wildnerness State Park

Harlow Lake, Escanaba River State Forest

Pounding Surf, Lake Superior, Keweenaw Peninsula

Gales of November, Lake Superior, Keweenaw Peninsula

Sunrise, Lake Superior, Keweenaw Peninsula

Gray Wolf

Maples and Chapel Falls, Pictured Rocks National Lakeshore

Grand Portal, Pictured Rocks National Lakeshore

Weathered Stump, Greenstone Ridge, Isle Royale National Park

Autumn Details

Presque Isle River, Porcupine Mountains Wildnerness State Park

Mud Lake, Keweenaw Peninsula

Aspens on Shoreline, Porcupine Mountains Wilderness State Park

Moonrise, Lake of the clouds, Porcupine Mountains Wilderness State Park

White Birch Forest, Pictured Rocks National Lakeshore

Aspen Leaf, Slate River, Huron Mountains

First Snow, Brockway Mountain

Cliff Edge, Brockway Mountain

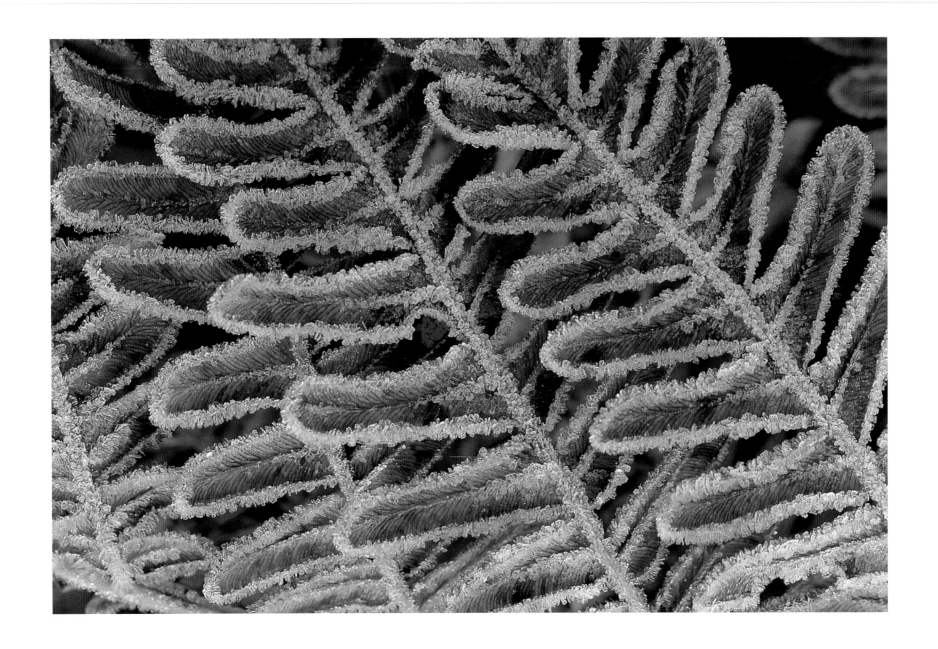

Frost on Fern, Seney National Wildlife Refuge

White-tailed Deer in Winter Yard

Crooked Lake, Sylvania Wilderness

Aspens, First Snow, Keweenaw Bay

Hoar Frost, Tahquamenon Falls State Park

Frozen Spray on Nine Bark Bush, Lake Superior

Snow-covered White Birch, Clark Lake, Sylvania Wilderness

Coyote Tracks on Rotten Ice, Sylvania Wilderness

Shore ice and splash, Lake Superior

Lake Superior Shore after Winter Storm

Fresh Snow, Cut River

White Birch in Snow

Drifted Snow, Copper Harbor

Fox Tracks in Snow, Craig Lake Wilderness

Presque Isle River, Porcupine Mountains State Park

Aurora Borealis, Tahquamenon Falls State Park

Ice Shards, Lake Superior

Pack Ice, Lake Superior

Sunset, Pack Ice, Lake Superior

Moonrise through Ice Window, Lake Superior

Sunset, Broken Pack Ice, Copper Harbor